Katy Perry

Jennifer Strand

abdopublishing.com

Published by Abdo Zoom™, PO Box 398166, Minneapolis, Minnesota 55439. Copyright © 2017 by Abdo Consulting Group, Inc. International copyrights reserved in all countries. No part of this book may be reproduced in any form without written permission from the publisher. Abdo Zoom™ is a trademark and logo of Abdo Consulting Group, Inc.

Printed in the United States of America, North Mankato, Minnesota
092016
012017

Cover Photo: Jordan Strauss/Invision/AP Images
Interior Photos: Jordan Strauss/Invision/AP Images, 1, 4; A. Ricardo/Shutterstock Images, 5; Sean Pavone/
Shutterstock Images, 6–7; Seth Poppel/Yearbook Library, 7; Shutterstock Images, 8, 14; S. Bukley/
Shutterstock Images, 9; Matt Sayles/AP Images, 10; Chris Pizzello/AP Images, 12; David Rowland/
Rex Features/AP Images, 13; Colombia Pictures/Photofest, 15; David J. Phillip/AP Images, 16–17; Helga Esteb/
Shutterstock Images, 18; Ding Zhenjie/Imaginechina/AP Images, 18–19

Editor: Emily Temple
Series Designer: Madeline Berger
Art Direction: Dorothy Toth

Publisher's Cataloging-in-Publication Data
Names: Strand, Jennifer, author.
Title: Katy Perry / by Jennifer Strand.
Description: Minneapolis, MN : Abdo Zoom, 2017. | Series: Stars of music |
    Includes bibliographical references and index.
Identifiers: LCCN 2016948678 | ISBN 9781680799194 (lib. bdg.) |
    ISBN 9781624025051 (ebook) | 9781624025617 (Read-to-me ebook)
Subjects: LCSH: Perry, Katy, 1984- --Juvenile literature. | Musician--United
    States--Biography--Juvenile literature. | Singers--United States--Biography--
    Juvenile literature.
Classification: DDC 782.42164092 [B]--dc23
LC record available at http://lccn.loc.gov/2016948678

Table of Contents

Katy Perry is a **popular** singer.
She has had many hit songs.

She is known for her fun costumes.

Early Life

Katy was born on October 25, 1984. She loved to sing. At age 16 she went to Nashville, Tennessee.

She met people in
the music business.

Rise to Fame

In 2001 Katy recorded an album. She was known as Katy Hudson then.

The album had Christian pop songs.
It did not sell very well.

In 2008 she changed her name to Katy Perry. She **released** a pop album. It was a hit!

Katy was **nominated** for a **Grammy Award**.

Then she went
on tour.

In 2010 Katy released her second pop album. It included the song "California Gurls."

Then she voiced Smurfette
in the movie *The Smurfs*.

Katy released another album in 2013.

16

Her song "Roar" topped the charts. She performed it at the Super Bowl.

Katy writes most of her music.
She releases hit after hit.

Her concerts have exciting effects. She wears colorful costumes, too.

Katy Perry

Born: October 25, 1984

Birthplace: Santa Barbara, California

Known For: Perry is a pop singer. Many of her songs are chart-topping hits.

1984: Katheryn Elizabeth Hudson is born on October 25.

1997: Katy gets a guitar for her birthday. She starts writing songs.

2001: Katy releases her first album. It is called *Katy Hudson*.

2008: Katy releases her first album as Katy Perry. It is called *One of the Boys*.

2010: Katy's second pop album is released.

2015: Katy performs at Super Bowl XLIX.

Glossary

Grammy Award – an important honor given out each year for music. There are many Grammy Awards.

nominated - formally made a candidate for an award.

popular - liked by many people.

released - made available to the public.

tour - when a band travels to different places to perform.